I LOVE YOU
JUST ENOUGH

By Robbyn Smith van Frankenhuyzen

Illustrated by Gijsbert van Frankenhuyzen

For Heather, a natural mother, then and now.

♥

ACKNOWLEDGMENTS

Our biggest thanks goes to our niece Keagan for her patience and enthusiasm while modeling as Heather. You are perfect in every way!

We also thank Becca and Dezra, Gray Bendall, and Jim Sikarskie, DVM. Finally, a huge thank-you to Victoria Monroe; we could not have done this book without you.

Sleeping Bear Press®
315 E. Eisenhower Parkway, Suite 200
Ann Arbor, MI 48108
www.sleepingbearpress.com

Printed and bound in the United States.

10 9 8 7 6 5 4 3 2 1

Library of Congress Cataloging-in-Publication Data

Frankenhuyzen, Robbyn Smith van.
I love you just enough / written by Robbyn Smith van Frankenhuyzen ;
illustrated by Gijsbert van Frankenhuyzen.
pages cm
Summary: "A young girl finds a baby wood duck separated from his family and teaches him to swim, hunt for bugs, and how to fly. She loved him just enough so that he could find his place in nature and return to his family"
— Provided by the publisher.
ISBN 978-1-58536-839-6
[1. Wood duck—Fiction. 2. Ducks—Fiction. 3. Wildlife rescue—Fiction.]
I. Frankenhuyzen, Gijsbert van, illustrator. II. Title.
PZ7.F8565Iam 2014
[E]—dc23   2013027776

AUTHOR'S NOTE

Wildlife rehabilitation on Hazel Ridge Farm was a family affair. As soon as our daughters, Heather and Kelly, were old enough to hold a bottle of milk for an orphaned animal or warm a chilled baby animal in their laps, they were eager to help. Heather had an innate ability to nurture an orphaned animal back to health. Her fearless and gentle touch seemed to calm a frightened animal.

Wood ducks are especially tricky ducks to raise because they frighten easily and in a panic may injure themselves. Heather's patience and devotion to the task of raising Mr. Peet was the perfect recipe for success. She learned responsibility, compassion, self-confidence, and a little heartbreak. These are life lessons she has carried with her to adulthood. We were proud of her then and are proud of her now.

We do not rehabilitate wildlife anymore, but for 25 years it was a big part of our lives. Conservation officers occasionally stopped by to inspect our facilities because the work requires state and federal permits. Nick built large cages that allowed plenty of room for the animals to run, fly, play, and chase. We repaired whatever was injured, raised orphans to survive on their own, and loved them just enough. Then we said goodbye. Wild animals are not meant to be pets. They belong in the wild.

—Robbyn and Gijsbert (Nick)

Today was the last day of school! Heather hopped off the bus and skipped up the gravel driveway. She was excited to spend the afternoon helping her dad in the prairie. The prairie was part of their farm—Hazel Ridge Farm.

"Let's go pull weeds," said Dad, and off they went.

Once in the prairie Heather settled in among the grasses and flowers to watch a spider weave her silky web.

"Look what I found," Heather said, holding up a fragile snake skin.

Heather gathered all the treasures that she had found— a sparkly stone that glittered gold, a piece of wood with beetle scribblings etched in it, a brown speckled eggshell and a red feather for her hair.

Pulling weeds was fun!

From the corner of her eye Heather saw
a fuzzy *something* move.

"Dad," she said quietly. "Come quick."

"What have you found now?" he asked.

"Shhh," Heather put her finger to her lips. "You'll scare him."

Hiding in a cluster of purple lupines was a frightened duckling.

"Now that is quite a treasure you've found," Dad said. "It looks like this little guy has been separated from his family."

"Will his family come back for him?" Heather asked. "Or can I take him home and be his family?"

"I don't know Heather. Taking care of a baby animal is a lot of responsibility," Dad explained. "You have to keep him safe and warm and fed. You have to teach him how to be a duck—to swim, to hunt for bugs, and how to fly."

"How will I teach him how to fly?" Heather asked.

"Well, we might have to rely on nature for that," Dad said with a smile.

"I will keep you safe," she said.

Then Dad put on his serious face. "The hardest thing that you will have to do is not to love him too much."

"I don't understand," Heather frowned. "Why can't I love him as big as I love you and Mom?"

"Loving him will be the easy part. This duckling will only be with us for a short while. His true family should be with other ducks. Saying goodbye will be hard," Dad said.

Heather looked at the helpless duckling and took a deep breath. "I think I can love him just enough, Dad."

Just then the duckling peeped, "Peet, peet, peet."

Heather scooped him up and giggled. "You even told me your name, little duck. I will call you Mr. Peet."

Back at home Heather asked, "What kind of duck is Mr. Peet?"

"Look at these tiny little claws on Mr. Peet's webbed feet," Dad pointed out. "Wood ducks nest in hollow trees or wood duck boxes, just like the boxes on our ponds. When the ducklings hatch they use those tiny claws to climb out of their nest."

An empty fish aquarium with a tight-fitting screen on top provided a safe place for Mr. Peet. He nestled under the heat lamp just as he would under his mother, content with his new home.

Dad knew that the ponds were the perfect place
to find tasty duck treats for Mr. Peet. As Dad
paddled the canoe, Heather scooped up all kinds
of squiggly things living in the pond.

Soon her bucket was overflowing with wiggly whirligigs, dragonfly larvae, crayfish, tadpoles, mosquito larvae, and more.

Every morning Heather filled a big bowl
with pond water and creatures. As
soon as Mr. Peet saw movement he
would hop in and begin eating
everything he could catch.

Mr. Peet splished and splashed and bathed and played. Heather
smiled. She took her job as mother duck very seriously.

Each day Heather lifted Mr. Peet from his aquarium home and set him on the floor. They played follow the leader. When he ran, his floppy, webbed feet flapped and slapped on the wood floor.

One day he ran so fast his feet lifted off the floor.

"You're a good duck," Heather cheered and Mr. Peet peeped.

"Let's see if he likes to swim in a big pond," Dad said one morning as he put Mr. Peet in the bathtub. The duckling swam and splashed and dipped and dived as Heather stayed close.

And so it went for many weeks. Mr. Peet explored every corner of the house, had a daily bathtub swim, and grew bigger every day.

He had even grown accustomed to helping Heather with her daily chores. She helped Mr. Peet to the top of the rabbit hutch so he could take in all sights. He watched as she fed the rabbits and the chickens and gave grain to the horse.

When the horse came too close, Mr. Peet made a fretful peet, peet.

"Have you had enough of chores?" she giggled.

Heather and Mr. Peet ran all around the farm. They ran when it was sunny. They ran when it was rainy. She always knew exactly where he was by the sound of his floppy feet and his flapping wings.

One day Heather ran ahead to chase a butterfly, leaving Mr. Peet behind. She turned around just in time to see Mr. Peet lift right off the ground and fly overhead.

"You did it," she called out.
"You can fly!"

It seemed to surprise Mr. Peet too.
He circled around, landing with a
clumsy plop at Heather's feet.

From then on Mr. Peet flew everywhere they went. Heather wondered how the ponds and woods and prairies looked from Mr. Peet's sky-high view. She imagined what it would be like to fly right next to Mr. Peet.

The warm summer days were perfect for swimming and fishing. Heather watched Mr. Peet dart for water bugs and minnows.

"Look at Mr. Peet, Dad. He doesn't need my help to find food anymore."

Dad smiled from the nearby dock as Heather and Mr. Peet splashed, bobbed, and floated.

One day after swimming, Mr. Peet wouldn't follow Heather and Dad from the pond like he usually did.

"Come on," she coaxed, "It's time to go home. It's not safe for you to be alone."

She tried to catch him, but he flew away.

Heather called and whistled and still no Mr. Peet.

"Daddy," Heather cried. "He's not ready to be on his own. Something might eat him."

Dad hugged her tight. "Mr. Peet knows where he belongs, and it's not on a farm."

Heather sniffled, "But he will be all by himself … in the dark."

Heather tried to be brave and not cry, but the sadness of Mr. Peet leaving was just too big.

The next morning while Heather was feeding the chickens, Mr. Peet surprised her by landing smoothly at her feet. "You came back!" she exclaimed.

"You silly duck. I was so worried. Where did you sleep last night?" Heather asked.

The dog sniffed the nearly full-grown duck
to welcome him home. Mr. Peet pinched his
nose, causing a yelp.

"I guess you can take care of yourself,"
Heather said to Mr. Peet.

Summer vacation ended and school began again. Heather returned to her school friends, and Mr. Peet found friends of his own.

She would see Mr. Peet at the pond now and again, but he stopped helping her with chores.

Dad had reminded her that she had done a wonderful
job raising Mr. Peet to be a strong and confident duck.
Heather's job was done, and now it was up to Mr. Peet.

She would need to trust that he would find safety in
a new family, a family of wood ducks just like him.

Shorter days and cooler nights meant birds of all kinds would begin their long journey south where the weather was warmer. Heather wondered if Mr. Peet would know to go with the other wood ducks.

Heather showed Dad on the calendar how many days since she last saw Mr. Peet.

"It has been ten days. Do you think he has flown south with his new family?" Heather asked.

"I am sure of it," Dad nodded. "You should be very proud of how you helped Mr. Peet."

Heather sighed. "Do you think I will ever see him again?

Dad paused and then said, "Ducks usually return to the place where they grew up. Mr. Peet may visit Hazel Ridge next spring. But if he doesn't, we'll know he found his own place in nature. He is not a farm duck anymore."

Heather hugged Dad a long time. She remembered all the things she did with Mr. Peet and felt proud.

"Daddy, I know Mr. Peet will be okay," she said, "because I loved him just enough."